DRUG—RESISTANT
SUPERBUGS

DRUG-RESISTANT SUPERBUGS

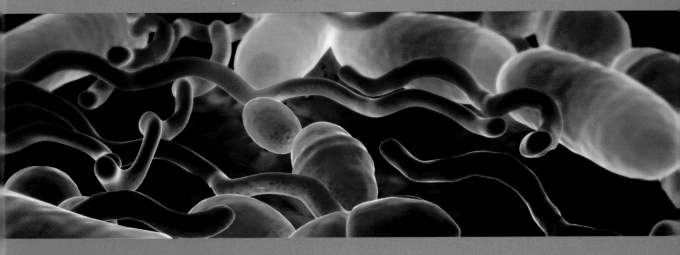

Lorrie Klosterman

 Marshall Cavendish
Benchmark
New York

With thanks to Adam J. Adler, PhD, Associate Professor, Center for Immunotherapy of Cancer and Infectious Diseases and Department of Immunology, University of Connecticut Health Center, for his expert review of the manuscript.

Marshall Cavendish Benchmark
99 White Plains Road
Tarrytown, New York 10591-5502
www.marshallcavendish.us

Library of Congress Cataloging-in-Publication Data

Klosterman, Lorrie.
Drug-resistant diseases and superbugs / by Lorrie Klosterman.
p. cm. — (Health alert)
Includes index.
Summary: "Provides comprehensive information on the causes, treatment, and history of drug-resistant diseases and superbugs"—Provided by the publisher.
ISBN 978-0-7614-3981-3
1. Drug resistance in microorganisms—Juvenile literature. 2. Bacteria—Juvenile literature. 3. Immune system—Juvenile literature. 4. Antibiotics—Juvenile literature. I. Title.
QR177.K56 2010
616.9'041—dc22

2008051241

Front Cover: E. coli bacteria
Title page: Various bacteria on a cellular surface

Photo research by Candlepants Incorporated
Cover Photo: Sebastian Kaulitzki / Alamy Images

The photographs in this book are used by permission and through the courtesy of:
Getty Images: 3D4Medical.com, 3; Dr. Fred Hossler, 14; Kay Blaschke, 16; David Scharf, 23; 24; P Barber - CMSP, 30; Dr. Dennis Kunkel, 35; Steven Puetzer, 41; Eric O'Connell, 43; Victoria Blackie, 48; Mark Adams, 56. *Photo Researchers Inc.*: Biomedical Imaging Unit, Southampton General Hospital, 5, 47; Dr P. Marazzi, 11; Roger Harris, 13; Juergen Berger, 17; Scimat, 18; Hank Morgan, 26; Mary Evans, 28. *Alamy Images*: Image Source Black, 8; Guy Croft SciTech, 21; foodfolio, 39; ImageDJ, 53. *AP Images*: Tim Ireland/PA Wire, 33; Andres Leighton, 51.

Editor: Joy Bean
Publisher: Michelle Bisson
Art Director: Anahid Hamparian

Printed in Malaysia

6 5 4 3 2 1

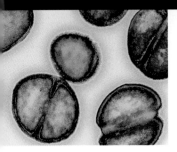

CONTENTS

1

WHAT IS IT LIKE TO HAVE A DRUG-RESISTANT SUPERBUG?

Summer vacation for Lee was not what he had hoped for. On the first Saturday of July, he fell off his bicycle while speeding through a gravel parking lot and scraped his knee badly. The wound seemed deep enough that his mother thought a doctor should look at it. Because it was a Saturday, the family's regular doctor's office was closed. So they went to the nearby hospital. The doctor cleaned the cut well and bandaged it.

Just a few days later, Lee started summer soccer camp, as he did every year. His knee bothered him a little because he had to bend it so often, and the bandage sometimes came off after hours of hard play in the summer sun. About a week after the bicycle accident, a scab had formed, but the skin around it was red, swollen, and warm to the touch. The following week,

Lee felt as if he was coming down with the flu. He had a fever, and his muscles ached. He felt too tired to go to camp. He admitted to his dad that his leg—the one he had scraped—was stiff and sore. He thought it might just be too much soccer practice, but he was beginning to worry that something was wrong. His dad started to worry as well.

Lee's dad took him to the doctor for a checkup. The doctor agreed that the injury should have healed more completely, and that Lee's fever and aches could be a sign that **bacteria** had gotten into the scrape and had begun to spread throughout his body. The doctor gave Lee some pills containing an **antibiotic** drug to stop the spread of bacteria. After two weeks of the antibiotic, though, Lee's leg hurt more than before, and he was feeling even sicker. The doctor gave Lee a different antibiotic to try.

By the middle of the summer, Lee's leg ached and he had trouble running and playing. His whole knee was red and swollen, and the scrape was damp again instead of scabbed over. Lee's doctor realized that Lee had a drug-resistant infection in his leg. Somehow, bacteria had gotten into the wound and had spread. The doctor put Lee in the hospital to get a different, very strong antibiotic. This drug was given **intravenously**—through a tiny tube that went into a blood vessel in his arm—to be sure it would get into his bloodstream and be carried all through his body.

Sometimes an ordinary cut will not get better on its own, and medical assistance is required to help it heal.

The stronger drug worked. Lee began to feel better in just a few days. By the end of summer, there seemed to be no trace of the infection left. Nobody ever figured out where he got the infection that took three antibiotics to cure. Even though he missed most of soccer camp, Lee was just glad to be feeling like his usual self. He could start school again, like everyone else.

2

WHAT ARE DRUG-RESISTANT SUPERBUGS?

The human body is great at healing itself from injuries and illnesses. Nearly everyone has had a cut or scrape that gets better and goes away on its own. Many common sicknesses, such as a cold or the flu, also go away after a few days or weeks. Healing happens as **cells** and chemicals in the body work together to repair injuries and to cure illnesses. Sometimes, though, **germs**—bacteria, **parasites**, or other tiny **microorganisms**—get into a wound, or they settle in the body somewhere and linger. Then healing may take a long time. A doctor's help and medications might be necessary, too.

INFECTION

When germs are living in a wound—or in some other part of the body where they are not supposed to be—it is called an

infection. An infected wound does not heal properly. The area around the wound becomes red, painful, and swollen. A white material called pus may collect in or around the wound. An infected wound might, over time, heal just fine. But it might get worse. Instead of healing, the germs can reproduce, making millions of copies of themselves that thrive in the warm, moist environment of the body. The germs spread into areas around the wound. They may even enter blood vessels and get carried

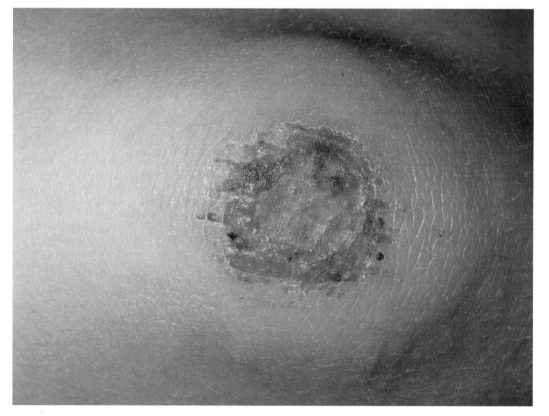

An infected scrape on a girl's knee shows a red and swollen area.

What Are Bacteria?

Powerful microscopes have allowed scientists to learn a lot about bacteria. Microscopes magnify objects and make them look hundreds or thousands of times larger than they really are. Some bacteria are round, some are rod-shaped (like a cucumber), and some are long and twisted. Each bacterium has a thin outer coating, or membrane, that holds it together. Some kinds of bacteria also have a tough cell wall outside the membrane and an outer capsule over that. Inside the bacterium is its genetic material, or DNA. All living things have DNA, which stores information needed to stay alive, to repair injured parts, and to reproduce. Surrounding the bacterium's DNA are many chemicals and tiny structures that do tasks, such as turning food into energy the bacterium can use to survive.

Some kinds of bacteria can move around. They have a long, hairlike strand that whips about or many shorter hairs that propel the bacterium along like oars on a boat. Bacteria that cannot move collect in groups wherever there is food and moisture. Most bacteria cannot live for more than a few hours or days outside a moist environment. But some are tough, and they can survive harsh conditions for years—possibly for centuries!

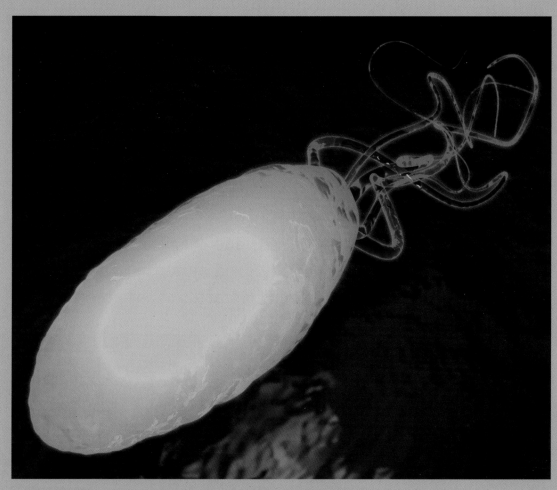

A rod-shaped bacterium with strands that help it move about in the body.

with the blood to distant parts of the body. A person with germs in his or her bloodstream gets dangerously ill because vital organs become infected. That is how an injury as simple as a cut finger can become a life-threatening problem.

Some of the most common diseases, or illnesses, are also caused by germs. A sore throat, a cold, the flu, ear infections, and a host of more serious ailments arise when these tiny organisms settle into the body.

THE IMMUNE SYSTEM

The body has a special team of cells and chemicals, called the **immune system**, that is especially good at getting rid of germs. The immune cells notice microorganisms, or other things that do not belong in the body, and destroy them. Some immune cells live in the bloodstream, where they are called **white blood cells** because they appear white when viewed with a microscope. White blood cells travel wherever blood goes,

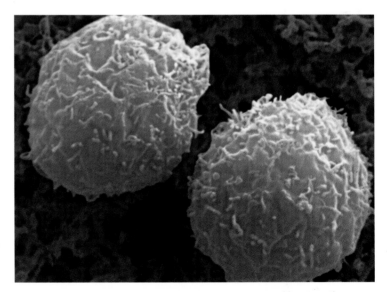

White blood cells as they appear when greatly magnified.

through millions of blood vessels that branch out into all parts of the body. White blood cells can squeeze their way out of blood vessels in their search for bacteria and other germs. When they find such invaders, the cells destroy them. The pus that collects at some wounds is made of white blood cells, fluid, and dead cells.

Besides white blood cells, there are millions of immune cells living among the body's other cells full-time instead of traveling in the bloodstream. Immune cells can be found in skin, in the moist linings of the mouth and throat, in the airways (tubes that carry air in and out of the lungs), in the digestive tract, in the brain, and in many other places. They are ready to attack any invaders they detect.

BOTHERSOME BACTERIA

There are thousands of different kinds of bacteria in the world. Most of them are harmless—or helpful—to people. Bacteria are plentiful all around us, in the air and soil, on things we touch and use, and on plants and animals. Bacteria live on human skin, as well as inside the mouth, nose, throat, and other moist places. Bacteria even live in our intestines, where they break apart plant foods that the human digestive system cannot take care of. Those bacteria make some useful vitamins that we need to stay healthy. Bacteria are a helpful and necessary part of life on Earth in countless ways.

Still, bacteria are more often to blame for germ-caused illnesses or infections than any other kind of microorganism. Bacteria that get into the intestines from polluted drinking water sicken and kill millions of people around the world. A bacterium called *Streptococcus pneumoniae*, which gets into airways and infects lungs, kills thousands of people around the globe each year.

This bacterium, Streptococcus pneumoniae, causes upper and lower respiratory infections.

Another kind of lung-infecting bacterium, *Mycobacterium tuberculosis*, causes the disease tuberculosis, or TB. Tuberculosis has been one of the world's greatest killers for centuries. Even though certain medications bring the bacteria under control, a lot of people in poor areas cannot get those medications. Tuberculosis remains one of the top causes of death in the world.

How Do Bacteria Harm Us?

Bacteria are many times smaller than the smallest human cell. Yet they can make us sick and even kill us. How can this be possible for such a tiny thing? One way bacteria harm us is by settling among healthy cells and robbing the cells of foods and nutrients they need to stay healthy and active. Another way bacteria can harm us is by making substances that injure nearby cells. These harmful substances, or toxins, can do a lot of damage because they break cells open, or eat away at the materials that hold cells together.

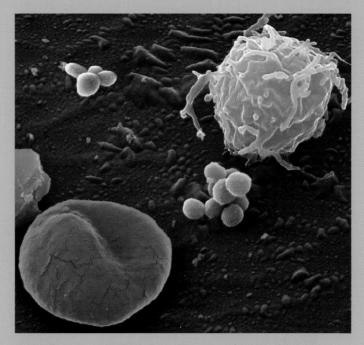

Bacteria are very tiny, even in comparison to human cells. Here, bacteria (yellow) are seen between red and white blood cells.

Bacteria get especially dangerous when they hide out where the body's germ-killing immune cells cannot easily find them. Some bacteria can enter cells and live inside them, hidden from immune cells that are on the lookout for invaders. Such bacteria may exit the cell again, but with a coating of material, or cloak, that surrounds the bacteria. Cloaked bacteria baffle immune cells, at least for a while, because they seem like tiny human cells instead of invaders.

Bacteria that are normally harmless can sicken people, too. For instance, bacteria that live inside the mouth without causing trouble can work their way deeper into the body and cause a sore throat or an ear infection. They can also cause much more serious infections if they get into the heart, brain, or kidneys. Bacteria called *Escherichia coli* (*E. coli*) live in the lower parts of our digestive tracts quite harmlessly—most of the time. But some kinds of *E. coli* can become deadly if they are eaten. *E. coli* are often found on meats because animals have these

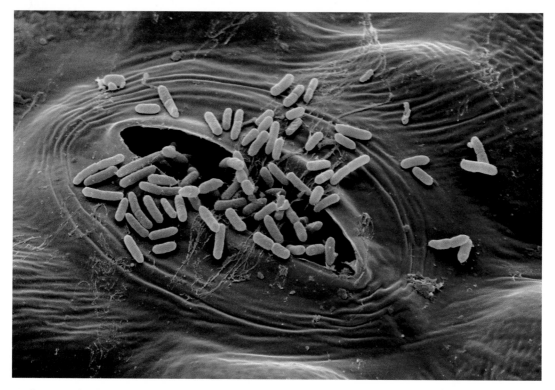

A close up look at E. coli on a lettuce leaf.

bacteria in their digestive tracts just as we do. The bacteria are in the animals' waste (feces), which can end up on the meat we eat. If the meat is not cleaned well enough or cooked to a temperature high enough to kill bacteria, the bacteria can enter people's bodies. *Salmonella enterica* bacteria, common in chicken feces and on chicken meat and eggs, also make people sick.

On farms or in the kitchen, bacteria from animal waste or contaminated meats can also get onto vegetables and fruits. About nine thousand people die of food contamination each year, mostly because of bacteria in meats. Many thousands more get sick and suffer days of terrible abdominal pains, vomiting, diarrhea, and other harsh symptoms before they recover.

HELP FROM THE DOCTOR

Even the immune system cannot stop every germ invasion. A doctor's help becomes very important when a wound is badly infected or germs have spread. Illnesses caused by germs may need medical attention, too. Pneumonia, for example, is a sickness in which bacteria or other microorganisms have gotten into the lungs. Lungs are the spongy organs in the chest that fill with air at each breath. Life-giving oxygen in that air crosses the lungs and gets into the bloodstream. The oxygen is then carried along in the blood to all parts of the body. The lungs of a person with pneumonia are infected with germs. The air sacs in the lungs fill with pus, mucus, and other liquids, and the lungs cannot function properly. Without medical care, pneumonia is often deadly.

Fortunately, a doctor can give medications that will destroy germs or keep them from spreading. Some medications work to halt bacteria, while others stop the spread of **viruses**. Yet others kill parasites. The medications used most often are those that kill bacteria or keep them from reproducing. Those medications are called antibiotics.

ANTIBIOTIC DRUGS

There are plenty of cleaners that kill bacteria or other germs on desktops, bathroom sinks, hospital equipment, and other objects. Many hand soaps contain bacteria-killing ingredients, too. But these cleaners would be poisonous, and would harm living cells, if they were used to kill bacteria inside people. Sick people need medications that do as little harm as possible to healthy cells while getting rid of germs.

Antibiotics work in different ways. Some antibiotics are good at stopping or killing several kinds of bacteria. Other antibiotics work on just one or a few similar kinds of bacteria. Antibiotic drugs are among the most important medical discoveries of all time. Today there are more than a hundred kinds that help people live through the same sorts of sicknesses and infections that killed millions of people in the past.

A problem has been growing over the last few decades, however. Bacteria have been changing so that they survive antibiotics. These are called **drug-resistant** bacteria. There was a time when it seemed people would be able to wipe out any disease-causing bacteria thanks to antibiotics. But bacteria have evolved with increasing exposure to common antibiotics, and a new struggle to beat drug-resistant bacteria is under way.

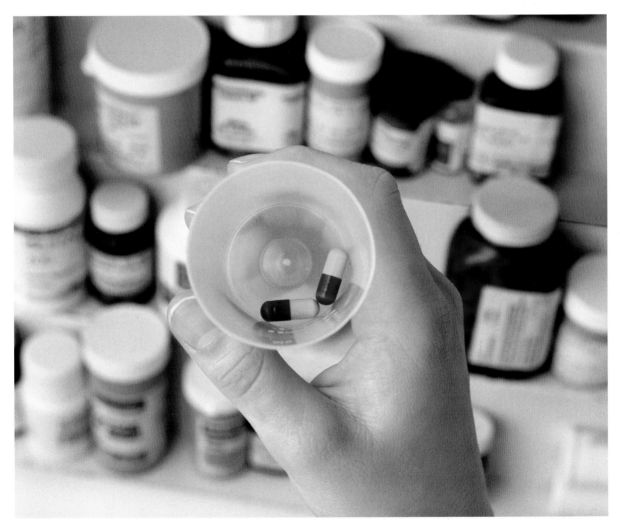

Antibiotics are prescribed by doctors to help kill bacteria in the body.

Viruses, Yeasts, Fungi, and Protozoa

Bacteria are not the only microscopic things that cause illness. Tiny structures called viruses also get into cells and spread, often destroying cells and making people ill. Viruses cause colds, influenza (the flu), and some other common illnesses.

Yeasts are tiny living organisms that thrive in moist places and are usually harmless. We even use them in foods to help make baked breads puffy and to create alcohol in beverages. But yeast sometimes thrives on the skin or on moist areas just inside the body's openings, such as the mouth and throat, where it causes itchiness and sores.

Fungi are simple living cells that can settle on moist skin or inside the body. Skin-loving fungi cause unpleasant conditions called athlete's foot and ringworm.

Protozoa are single-celled organisms that are plentiful in soil and water. They get inside the body and settle in organs or among the body's cells, damaging them and using up food and vitamins. Malaria and intestinal infections are examples of dangerous illnesses caused by protozoa. Each of these kinds of microorganisms can be treated with medications. But, as with bacteria, some protozoa have become resistant to drugs that are used to kill them.

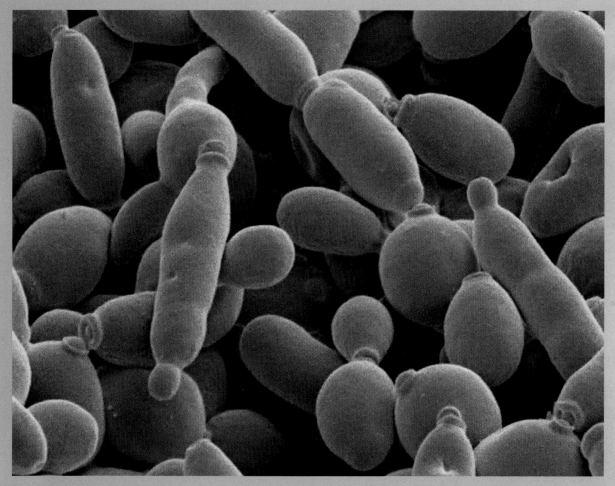

Yeast cells.

BACTERIA FIGHT BACK

Alexander Fleming, along with some other experts who helped create antibiotic medications, predicted that one day bacteria would be able to survive the drugs. Fleming had noticed that some of the bacteria he was studying flourished even after being treated with an antibiotic that should have killed them. He tried adding more of the antibiotic, and he found that a

Alexander Fleming is most famous for his discovery of the antibiotic powers of penicillin in 1928. He shared the 1945 Nobel Prize for Physiology or Medicine with the two chemists who had perfected a method of producing penicillin.

very high dose could stop them. But that amount would be too high to give a patient safely.

Today, many bacterial **strains** survive treatment with drugs that once stopped them. Strains are groups of bacteria of a certain kind that are a little different from the rest of their kind. How do drug-resistant strains arise? It takes two steps. First, a bacterium's DNA must change, or **mutate**. DNA holds all the information about what the bacterium is made of, how it lives, and how it reproduces. If that information mutates, the bacterium becomes different somehow. Mutations happen all the time. Some mutations have made it possible for bacteria to withstand drugs.

For example, some antibiotic drugs keep a bacterium from building its cell wall properly. Without a good cell wall, the bacterium is weak and dies easily. But a mutated bacterium could have different information in its DNA that causes the cell wall to be built differently, and the drug cannot affect it. Another example is that some mutated bacteria have found a way to destroy the drug so rapidly that it cannot harm them. Other bacteria are able to pump the drug back out of them as soon as it gets inside.

DRUG-RESISTANT STRAINS AND SUPERBUGS

A mutated bacterium can easily lead to a whole strain of drug-resistant bacteria. The bacterium can simply make many copies of itself. Each of those copies will have the mutation, too, and can survive even when medication is taken. Some bacteria can copy bits of their DNA and exchange them with other bacteria; this spreads the mutation around. Bacteria are also good at snatching up DNA from dead and broken bacteria. Another way that mutated DNA gets spread around is through viruses. Viruses can attach to a bacterium and pick up DNA, then move on to another bacterium and leave the DNA there.

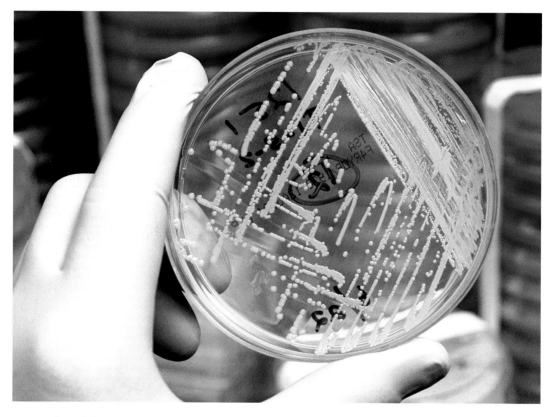

Rows of antibiotic resistant bacteria grown in a Petri dish.

Each of these ways of passing on DNA can create drug-resistant strains.

Over time, a strain of bacteria can collect a number of different mutations. This makes it resistant to many antibiotics. Such a strain of bacteria is called a **superbug**. If a person gets infected with a superbug, the immune system might still be able to get rid of it just fine. But if the immune system cannot get rid of the superbug, it will be difficult to find an antibiotic to stop the bacteria. Superbugs can do a lot of damage to a person's body before a cure is found. A doctor may try many different antibiotics for weeks or months in the hope that something will work. Sometimes the search fails, and the person dies.

Superbugs are one of the world's greatest health concerns. Some of them are spread among people by sneezing, coughing, or touching the infected area of another person. Health experts are coming up with all kinds of ideas about how to prevent the spread of superbugs, how to help people who have them, and how to prevent more of them from developing.

3

THE HISTORY OF DRUG-RESISTANT SUPERBUGS

In the late 1600s, Anton van Leeuwenhoek built better lenses for microscopes and with better lenses, discovered bacteria.

The history of superbugs begins centuries ago, at a time when nobody knew what caused illnesses. Bacteria, viruses, and other microorganisms were far too tiny to see. But in the 1670s, a Dutch merchant named Anton van Leeuwenhoek discovered a whole new world of microscopic objects. At first he was only interested in looking closely at the quality of fabrics that he bought and sold. He used curved glass lenses to magnify their threads so that he could study the fabric well. The glass lenses enlarged what he saw, just as a curved drop of water magnifies the surface it rests on.

Leeuwenhoek soon learned to make better lenses. He also created microscopes to hold lenses in such a way that he could magnify things a few hundred times their real size. That made it possible to see objects that had been invisible to the human eye until then. With his microscopes, Leeuwenhoek noticed tiny little specks everywhere. There were millions and millions of them. The specks could even spilt in two, and within hours they could make many more of themselves. Some kinds were able to move around. Leeuwenhoek had discovered bacteria.

Scientists at the time were fascinated by these new "animacules," as they were called then. But nobody imagined that something so small as bacteria could be dangerous to one's health. It was much later that bacteria and illness were linked clearly. In the late 1800s, a French chemist, Louis Pasteur, figured out that bacteria caused a deadly disease called anthrax. At about the same time, a German doctor, Robert Koch, and his coworkers invented ways to keep bacteria alive in the laboratory so they could study them closely. They took samples of saliva, blood, or other liquids from sick people and animals. Then they grew colonies of bacteria in the samples. Koch's coworker, Julius Petri, invented a flat glass dish with a glass top to hold the **agar** on which bacteria would grow, and to view the bacteria spreading across it. To this day, **microbiologists**, who study bacteria and other microorganisms, use glass or plastic Petri dishes filled with agar.

The studies of Pasteur, Koch, Petri, and others made it clear that bacteria could sicken and kill people.

MAKING MEDICATIONS

The next important event in the history of superbugs was the creation of medications that cure bacterial illnesses. One such drug, created in the early 1900s, had arsenic in it. Arsenic kills bacteria, but it is poisonous and can make people quite sick. In the 1930s, chemicals called sulfa drugs were created, and they became very popular for treating all kinds of sicknesses and infections. They are still used today—but not often, because bacteria have become resistant to them.

The next important antibiotic, **penicillin**, was discovered by chance. Alexander Fleming, a Scottish researcher working in the 1920s, is credited with noticing that mold called *Penicillium notatum*

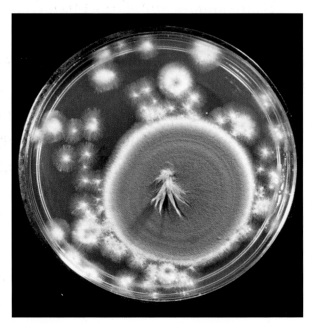

Penicillin mold growing in a Petri dish.

could keep bacteria from growing next to it. History says that some mold accidentally started growing near the bacteria Fleming was studying. Around the mold was a patch where no bacteria were visible. With careful studies, Fleming was able to prove that a liquid made by the mold was a bacteria-blocking substance. He named the liquid penicillin.

It was ten more years before scientists tested penicillin as a medication. Mice were the first test subjects. In Britain, researchers gave a group of mice a shot of deadly bacteria. Then they gave a few of the mice penicillin as well. The scientists found that the mice that got both bacteria and penicillin survived, while the mice that did not get penicillin died of the bacterial infection.

Even though penicillin proved helpful in mice, scientists were afraid to try the same kind of test on human beings. But by the 1940s, World War II was under way, and injured soldiers were dying of infected wounds. One of the penicillin researchers, Howard Florey, traveled to the war zone and took penicillin with him. He gave it to the wounded soldiers, and it worked like a miracle. Penicillin saved thousands of lives during the war, and it has saved millions since then. Fleming, Florey, and a coworker, Ernst Boris Chain, all were awarded the Nobel Prize in 1945 for their remarkable work in discovering penicillin.

In the early 1900s, it was not easy to make large amounts of penicillin that worked properly. Large **pharmaceutical companies** helped out by inventing ways to make pure,

Superbugs in the Hospital

Hospitals are places where people go to get well, but there is a growing problem: More and more people are getting sick with infections they get while in the hospital. An elderly woman, for instance, may be in the hospital to have a broken hip repaired, but during her recovery she becomes ill with pneumonia. Each hospital does its best to keep everything germ-free by using **disinfectants**, but patients can still get bacteria from furniture, equipment, doors, or other objects. In addition, bacteria can travel in hospital air in tiny droplets of moisture from coughing or sneezing patients. Doctors and nurses may also unknowingly carry bacteria from patient to patient.

Some of the bacteria found in hospitals are superbugs. One example is MRSA (pronounced "mersa"), which stands for methicillin-resistant *Staphylococcus aureus*. Methicillin is another drug in a long line of antibiotics that no longer stamp out these bacteria. A few decades ago, MRSA was found only in hospitals. Today the bacteria show up outside hospitals and can kill people who become infected—even healthy athletes have fallen prey to MRSA. In the United States, about 90,000 people a year get infected, and about 19,000 people die of MRSA.

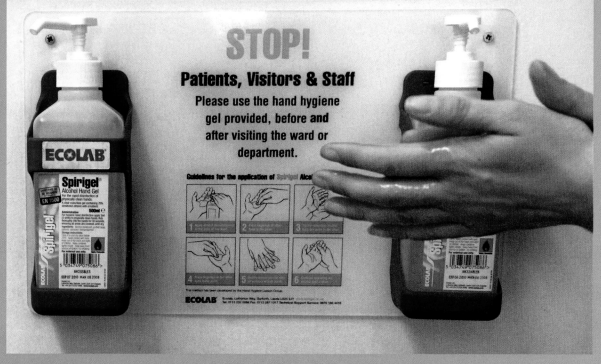

Hospitals try to keep germs from transferring from patient to patient by installing disinfectants on the walls for all to use.

long-lasting penicillin. Now there are many pharmaceutical companies making hundreds of antibiotic medications. But time has shown that for each new drug they create, sooner or later bacteria start to resist it.

THE RISE OF SUPERBUGS

Toward the end of the 1990s, drug-resistant bacteria were getting noticed. At first they were thought to be rare, and something few people needed to worry about. Today, it is a different story. Diseases that have not been a worry for many years are once again a cause for concern. Dozens of strains of bacteria are resistant to at least one drug. They can infect the ears, nose, throat, skin, blood, lungs, kidneys, brain, heart, and other organs. A few superbugs are especially dangerous because they do not respond to any antibiotics at all.

Not only bacteria, but also viruses and protozoa are becoming resistant to the drugs that used to stop them or slow their spread. Those microorganisms can cause deadly diseases, too, such as AIDS (autoimmune deficiency syndrome), malaria, and many others.

MEDICATIONS WORKING AGAINST US

Medical experts agree that drug-resistant germs have become such a problem partly because medications are being used incorrectly. Some people are not taking them for a long enough period of time. For instance, a sick person might take

Doctors may be contributing to the growth of superbugs by giving patients antibiotics even when the doctor does not know what is wrong with the patient.

a medication for just a few days and then stop because he or she feels better. The drug may already have killed many of the germs—the weakest ones—but the stronger ones are left to survive and spread. The person gets sick again, but this time with resistant bacteria. The medication will not work well again. Instead, a stronger one will be needed to kill the spreading bacteria. In the meantime, those bacteria can be spread to other people.

Another problem is that doctors often give antibiotics to patients without knowing what is causing an illness. Doctors do this because they want to help patients get better fast, and they may even be trying to save a patient's life. Otherwise, they would have to wait for several days while doctors run laboratory tests to identify what is wrong. So sometimes doctors guess at what germs are to blame, and they give the patient a medication that might work. Patients who are given antibiotics sometimes turn out to have a viral infection. Antibiotics do nothing to kill viruses—but in the meantime, the drug may have killed off harmless bacteria and left room for drug-resistant ones to spread.

THE MEAT CONNECTION

Our food supply is also a part of the drug-resistance problem. The animals we eat, such as cows, pigs, sheep, and chickens, are often given antibiotics like the ones people take. In fact, more than half of the antibiotics used in the United States go to food animals instead of people. Unfortunately, a good deal of the antibiotics are given to healthy animals, not sick ones. For years, farmers have been putting small amounts of antibiotics in animals' feed because it makes them grow fatter (though it is not clear why). Also, farmers who raise animals in crowded conditions often give them antibiotics to prevent sickness.

Using antibiotics in these ways kills off weak bacteria, while drug-resistant bacteria flourish in the animals. The antibiotic-resistant strains then spread to people. For example, people sometimes become ill with *Campylobacter* bacteria after eating undercooked chicken. Antibiotics can help them to get better. But in 1995, farmers started putting in their chicken feed an antibiotic that doctors use to treat people. Now, *Campylobacter* bacteria that are resistant to that antibiotic have been turning up in sick people, and doctors need to find a different medication to help them.

On many farms, animals are packed so tightly together that they can hardly move around. This allows diseases—and drug-resistant bacteria—to spread easily. Studies have shown that simply giving animals more room to roam keeps them healthier without medications.

LIVING IN A DRUG-RESISTANT WORLD

A few decades ago, drug companies became less interested in making new antibiotics. After all, the ones they had already created seemed to work very well. Infections that once killed people were almost never seen—at least not in countries where people could get good health care and medications. Now it is clear that humans have not won the war on germs, as it once seemed.

With the rise of drug-resistant bacteria and other germs, some companies are getting more interested in inventing new drugs. Microbiologists are busy looking for new ways to destroy germs. Health workers are trying better ways to keep germs from spreading. Many of the world's nations are getting together to plan what each can do to improve the health of its citizens and to stop the spread of germs.

Most Chicken Meat Has Germs

A magazine called *Consumer Reports* provides information about things that average people might want to know about. For instance, every so often the magazine has researchers test chicken meat for bacteria, so that shoppers understand that food contamination is a big problem. The magazine's 2006 contamination test found the worst news yet. Eighty-three percent of the raw chickens that were from grocery stores had *Campylobacter* or *Salmonella* bacteria. Many chickens had both types of bacteria.

Meat with bacteria looks the same, and smells the same as the clean meat. The researchers also tested the bacteria to see if they could resist the antibiotics a doctor would use to treat someone sickened by eating the meat. Sixty-seven percent of the *Campylobacter* bacteria were resistant to one or more medications. Eighty-four percent of the *Salmonella* bacteria were resistant to medications. These astounding numbers are a reminder that raw meat must be handled and cooked very carefully to keep people from getting sick. Even a tiny, invisible drop of moisture from raw meat can cause food poisoning.

Chicken meat must be handled and cooked carefully in order to make sure all bacteria in it is killed.

4

DIAGNOSING, TREATING, AND COPING WITH DRUG-RESISTANT DISEASES

Medical experts know that drug-resistant diseases are going to be around for quite a while. The fight between medications and germs will go on, maybe forever. But some simple steps will help slow the spread of germs and superbugs. Everybody has a part to play.

KEEPING CLEAN

One way to lower the chances of getting a superbug—or any germ-caused illness—is to have good personal hygiene. Wash your hands with soap and warm water before meals or snacks, and after using the bathroom. It is not necessary to wash with a bacteria-killing soap. Health experts believe that these soaps

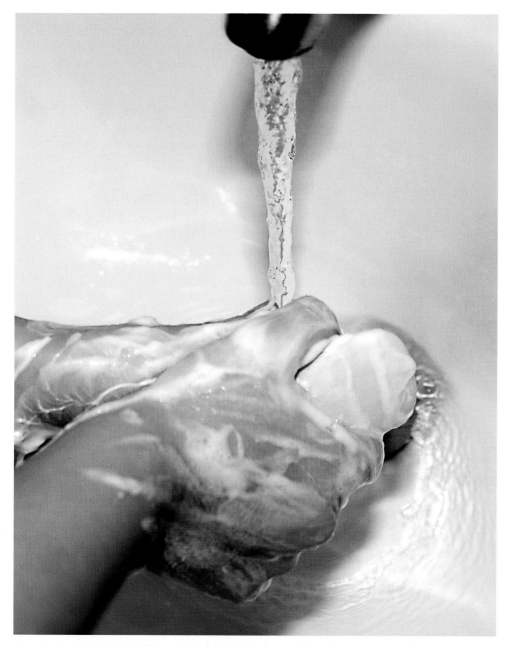

Washing your hands before eating helps to keep bacteria from entering your body from your hands.

Good Habits with Foods

....

Thousands of people die each year, and millions more get sick, because of bacteria in food, especially undercooked meats. Here are some safety tips for proper cooking and handling of animal foods:

- Never eat raw animal foods (beef, pork, chicken, sheep, fish, shellfish, eggs, milk) or uncooked foods made of them (such as cookie dough containing raw eggs).
- Wash your hands immediately after handling any kind of raw animal foods.
- Clean up spilled animal foods right away with disposable towels.
- Never prepare fruits or other foods that will be eaten raw using the same cutting boards, dishes, and utensils that were used with raw animal foods and have not yet been washed.
- Cook meats thoroughly to kill any bacteria. Use a meat thermometer to be sure these temperatures are reached inside the meats: 145 degrees Fahrenheit (63 degrees Celsius for beefsteaks and roasts, 160 °F (71°C) for beef patties and any kind of pork, and 160 °F for chicken.
- Keep cooked meat hot until it is served.
- Refrigerate leftovers right away, but throw out any cooked meats that have been at room temperature for more than two hours.
- Never recook meat that has been partly cooked and then left out for a while.

A meat thermometer will tell you if your food has been cooked thoroughly.

are making the superbug problem worse by giving bacteria yet another chemical that will not kill them. Ordinary soap and water works very well to kill bacteria, if used properly. Wash for about half a minute and then use a dry towel—not one that has been hanging around damp for days.

People can pass bacteria around in public bathrooms, schools, playgrounds, locker rooms, cafeterias, swimming pool areas, and even hospitals. It is a good idea to wash your hands and face after being in these places. Always wear shoes of some kind in public changing rooms and bathrooms. At swimming areas, do not swallow the water, whether you are at a stream, a pond, a lake, or a swimming pool—even your backyard kiddie pool.

DIAGNOSING A DRUG-RESISTANT DISEASE

Even people who practice good hygiene are going to pick up germs sometimes. The immune system will often destroy the germs. But if a cut or scrape gets swollen, red, painful, and warm to the touch, or if it gets much worse in just a few hours, it may be getting dangerously infected. A doctor should look at it right away. The immune system is usually good at clearing out germs that cause illnesses, too. Even as the immune system does its job, a sick person may feel nauseous, tired, stiff, and sore, and may develop a fever. Other signs of germ-caused sicknesses are headaches, stomach pains or other harsh pain, vomiting, and diarrhea. If an illness does not get better in a few days, or if any symptom gets much worse in just a few hours, it is important to see a doctor right away. A doctor's job is to make a **diagnosis**—to determine the likely cause of illness or injury. Doctors look carefully at their patients. They may take a blood or urine sample or do other tests to figure out what is wrong.

TREATMENT

Someone with a healthy immune system can probably destroy drug-resistant bacteria. The danger is when the immune system fails. Infants do not have very strong immune systems. Older people tend to have weaker immune systems. Also, some people have diseases that lower their natural germ-fighting ability. Those people need help fighting off infections. In addition, some germs spread and cause damage to the body very quickly—before even a powerful immune system can destroy them.

A doctor may choose an antibiotic for the patient to try for a few weeks in the hope that bacteria are the problem and the chosen drug will work. A doctor who knows about superbugs also understands that giving antibiotics too often helps create superbugs. So a doctor must make the hard decision of whether to give an antibiotic drug right away or to wait and see if the person gets better without one. Doctors know that viruses and other kinds of germs can cause the same symptoms as bacteria.

A Sampling of Superbug Bacteria

Dozens of strains of bacteria are resistant to more than one drug that is used to stop them. Here are examples of some of the most dangerous bacterial superbugs today.

Superbug	Main Health Problem
MRSA (methicillin-resistant *Staphylococcus aureus*); resists several drugs, including the newest one that used to work, methicillin	skin and organ infections
VRE (vancomycin-resistant *Enterococcifaecium* bacteria); resistant to several antibiotics	infections of internal organs and wounds
E. coli 0157; sickens about 70,000 people in the United States each year	food poisoning; (sometimes called hamburger disease), with very bad stomach pains, bloody diarrhea, vomiting, and sometimes kidney damage
Salmonella typhimurium DT104; resists at least five antibiotics	food poisoning (usually from chicken or eggs), with bad stomach pains, diarrhea, and vomiting

Superbug	Main Health Problem
MDR TB (multidrug-resistant tuberculosis), a strain of *Mycobacterium tuberculosis* resistant to two antibiotics	tuberculosis, a life-threatening lung infection that kills millions of people yearly
XDR TB (extensively drug-resistant tuberculosis); resists all antibiotics	tuberculosis

MRSA bacteria are resistant to many commonly prescribed antibiotics.

If they prescribe an antibiotic to someone who has a virus, the drug will be useless. Worse yet, it could help drug-resistant bacteria take hold.

Because of drug resistance, doctors who treat children with common ailments such as ear infections or sore throats are not giving antibiotics as much as they once did. Most children get better on their own. And in some cases, viruses are to blame. Still, parents sometimes get angry with their doctor for not providing antibiotics. They need to understand how serious the problem of drug resistance is.

Taking antibiotics can cause some side effects for some people.

THE DOWNSIDES OF ANTIBIOTICS

Antibiotics are not perfect drugs. Like all medications, they have **side effects**. A common side effect of antibiotics is nausea. Some people feel so ill when they take certain antibiotics that they stop taking them. There are many other possible side effects of taking antibiotics. If taken for many weeks or months, they can harm vital organs. Some people are **allergic** to antibiotics. An allergy can be mild, causing little more than an annoying skin rash. But powerful allergic reactions can become medical emergencies. The antibiotic can cause the airways to narrow, making it very hard to breathe. An allergic reaction to an antibiotic can be deadly.

These downsides of antibiotics (and of other germ-killing medications as well) make doctors cautious about prescribing them. Some of the best germ-killing drugs are also the ones that make people feel sickest. So a doctor must weigh the pros and cons of giving a certain drug. It may be best to first try a medication that has the least side effects, to see if that clears up the infection.

WHEN THE PROBLEM IS A SUPERBUG

With superbugs, the usual medications do not help. At first a doctor is not likely to know that an infection is caused by a superbug. But if a patient has been taking a medication for some weeks and is not getting better, the doctor might begin to suspect that a drug-resistant germ is at work. The doctor probably will try a different medication, and then maybe another. In the meantime, laboratory tests may have indicated what type of germ it is.

During that time, the patient could become very ill and possibly be put in the hospital for the best care. Antibiotics or other medications might be given intravenously, Then it will be certain that a high dose of the drug gets into the person's bloodstream and is carried everywhere in the body. Hopefully, the medication will finally kill the germs. If not, the immune system may still win the battle, with the help of good medical care. But in some cases, there is no way to completely get rid of the superbug, and the patient dies.

In many parts of the world, good medical care is hard to find. People in poorer countries often die of illnesses that almost never kill people in wealthier countries with better medical care. A leading cause of death for many of the world's citizens is infections they get from unclean drinking water. The people often have weak immune systems because they do not get enough food. They may have other illnesses that harm their immune cells. In addition, the water and soil may have large numbers of germs because of poor sanitation. There may be no toilets, so that human waste collects near water supplies. Garbage collects, too, and gives germs food to thrive on.

When people who live in these conditions do get sick, medications could easily clear up the infection. But many people live in the countryside, far from towns or cities that have doctors. Even if there is a doctor nearby, he or she will probably have only a few medications on hand. The spread of superbugs is especially dangerous among poor communities. There is little a doctor can do. Sadly, superbugs are showing up in these places, and they are deadly.

Polluted water in Santo Domingo, Dominican Republic, causes a number of illnesses each year.

BUILDING A STRONG IMMUNE SYSTEM

Everyone gets sick now and then, and a strong immune system fights back and wins. With a strong immune system, medications to kill germs are unnecessary. One way to avoid having to deal with a drug-resistant illness is to take good care of your immune system. Be sure to eat nutritious foods as often as you can. Each day have some foods that are rich in vitamins and minerals, such as whole grains and fresh or lightly cooked vegetables and fruits, especially brightly colored ones (often the colors are useful nutrients). Taking vitamins can help, but it is really best to eat vitamin-rich foods instead. Eat only small amounts of foods with lots of sugar. These work against the immune system's efforts because microorganisms thrive on sugar.

Doing activities that get your body moving is also good for your immune system. Exercise makes your heart pump faster and blood flow better. That, in turn, helps send white blood cells on a bodywide search for germs. It also helps the blood to wash toxins and debris from among cells and clear them away. Many scientific studies have shown that people who get some exercise nearly every day are healthier than people who do not exercise regularly. The activity can be something as easy as riding a bike, playing ball, taking the dog for a walk, or even doing some cleaning around the house.

A healthy diet with plenty of fruits and vegetables helps keep your immune system in good working order.

YOUR JOB: USE ANTIBIOTICS CORRECTLY AND SAFELY

If antibiotics are used the wrong way, they can actually help create resistant bacteria. Patients need to take antibiotics properly. Here is what you can do to help slow the spread of superbugs.

- Take a medication for as long as a doctor says to. People sometimes stop taking a drug after a few days because they feel better. But the medication must still do its job for many more days in order to get rid of all traces of germs.

- Do not skip a dose of medication. Pills or liquid drugs are meant to be taken once or twice a day, perhaps more often. It is important to take every dose, and to do so on time. This makes sure the amount of the drug builds up to a high level in the body.

- Ask your doctor what might happen if you have an allergic reaction to the drug. Be alert for any changes. Call the doctor right away if a reaction begins, or even if you wonder about it. It could save your life.

- Never leave any medication containers in places where young children can get to them.

- Sometimes there are a few pills or liquid medication left over after taking all of what the doctor prescribed. Never throw the leftover medication down the drain. Close the container tightly and throw it in the garbage where no one else can get to it.

- Do not use a medication that someone else has given you, even if it appears to be exactly the same medication as the one prescribed to you. Only use the container you got for your own illness. Someone else's could be a different drug or a different amount per pill. It could be old and weak.

TOMORROW'S HOPE

Health experts agree that superbugs are not going away anytime soon. Because of this, doctors, researchers, health organizations, community groups, and governments are all working to learn about superbugs and how to stop their spread. Some global organizations, such as the World Health Organization, are helping to organize efforts by many countries to join in the fight against superbugs. One of the main goals is to improve medical care and sanitation in poor countries. Another is to **vaccinate** people to prevent them from getting sick with certain deadly illnesses in the first place. Children who are vaccinated at a young age will be protected from some of the diseases that now have superbug strains, such as tuberculosis.

In the United States, the Centers for Disease Control and Prevention (CDC), which is part of the federal government, is going to collect better information about all kinds of illnesses, including how many people have drug-resistant strains. The CDC is also going to get more research under way to understand just how bacteria avoid being killed by medications. In addition,

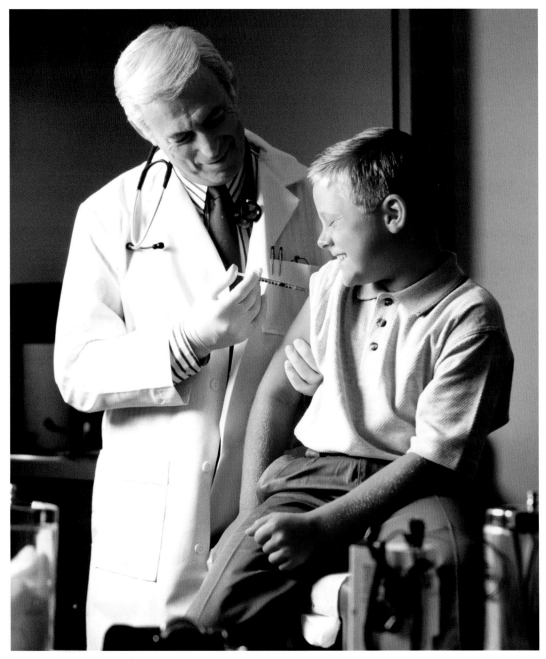

Getting vaccinated can stop you from getting some harmful illnesses.

CDC officials will continue to educate everyone about ways to keep superbugs from spreading.

There is a lot that you can do, too. Good hygiene, watching for signs of infections and illness that are not getting better, and using medications properly are very important—and easy to do. With people doing their part, and with researchers and doctors doing theirs, we can overcome the challenge of superbugs.

GLOSSARY

agar—A gelling substance used in foods.

allergic—Likely to experience a reaction to a drug or other substance. This reaction can be annoying, dangerous, or even deadly.

antibiotic—A drug that kills bacteria or stops them from spreading.

bacteria (plural of bacterium)—Tiny, single-celled organisms that are nearly everywhere. Some cause infections and illnesses.

cells—The smallest living units of an organism.

diagnosis—A doctor's determination about what kind of sickness a person has.

disinfectant—A chemical that destroys some forms of harmful microorganisms.

drug-resistant—Able to survive a medication intended to kill germs.

germs—Microorganisms that cause illness. Examples are bacteria, viruses, and protozoa.

immune system—The body's team of cells and chemicals that work together to destroy viruses, bacteria, and other things that cause infection or illness.

infection—An area of the body that has been taken over by harmful bacteria, viruses, parasites, or other germs.

intravenously—Given through a tube directly into a vein.

microbiologists—Researchers who specialize in studying bacteria, viruses, and other microorganisms.

microorganisms—Organisms that are so tiny they can only be seen with the aid of a microscope.

mutate—To undergo a permanent change.

parasite—An organism that lives off another organism.

penicillin—A medication that began the antibiotic era of medicine.

pharmaceutical companies—Companies that make drugs.

protozoa—Single-celled organisms, some of which cause illnesses.

side effects—Unwanted changes in the body caused by a drug.

strains—Groups of bacteria that are a little different from other bacteria of the same kind.

superbug—A germ that survives two or more medications that are used to stop it.

vaccinate—To give a person a shot, usually of a weakened or inactive germ, which makes the immune system better at fighting off active forms of the same germ.

viruses—Tiny structures, smaller than bacteria, that sometimes cause disease.

white blood cells—Cells that are part of the immune system and that find and destroy germs.

FIND OUT MORE

Books

Klosterman, Lorrie. *The Immune System*. New York: Benchmark Books, 2008.

Kornberg, Arthur. *Germ Stories*. New York: University Science Books, 2007.

Reh, Beth Donovan. *Germs*. New York: Thompson Gale, 2005.

Townsend, John. *Pox, Pus & Plague: A History of Disease and Infection*. Chicago: Raintree, 2006.

Websites

Centers for Disease Control and Prevention: About Antibiotic Resistance
http://www.cdc.gov/drugresistance/community/anitbiotic-resistance-faqs.htm

Centers for Disease Control and Prevention: Get Smart: What Everyone Should Know and Do
http://www.cdc.gov/drugresistance/community/know-and-do.htm

KidsHealth: Food Poisoning
http://kidshealth.org/kid/ill_injure/sick/food_poisoning.html

KidsHealth: What Are Germs?
http://kidshealth.org/kid/talk/qa/germs.html

INDEX

Page numbers in **bold** are illustrations.